A book
*is a present you can open
again and again.*

THIS BOOK BELONGS TO

_____

FROM

_____

All About How Things Are Made

with Inspector McQ

Written by Kathleen Kain
Illustrated by Robert Byrd

World Book, Inc.
a Scott Fetzer company
Chicago London Sydney Toronto

Copyright © 1992
World Book, Inc.
525 West Monroe Street
Chicago, Illinois 60661

Printed in the United States of America
ISBN 0-7166-1627-0
Library of Congress Catalog Card No. 91-65756

A/IA

Cover design by Rosa Cabrera
Book design by George Wenzel
Inspector McQ illustrated by Eileen Mueller Neill
Photos, pages 6-7, © Binney & Smith, Inc.
Photos, pages 10-11, © James River Corp.
World Book photo, page 12
World Book photo, page 14
World Book photo, page 17, Bresler Ice Cream Company
Photo, page 19, © Michael Hintlian
Photo, page 22, Lotto Italia
Photo, page 23, © Roy Morsch, The Stock Market
World Book photos, page 25, John R. Hamilton, Globe
Photo, page 25 (bottom), reprinted by permission of UFS, Inc.
Photo, page 27, Tony Friedkin from Salisbury Communications

Step into my office. The name's Inspector McQuestion, but you may call me McQ. I've heard you've got questions. Well, my job is finding the answers. Sure, you can tag along. But keep your eyes open—in case a clue just happens to drop out of the blue.

How are lead pencils made?

This answer may take some digging because the "leads" in pencils are not lead at all. They are thin sticks of graphite.

Let's visit a pencil factory. A blender mixes ground-up graphite with clay and water. The more graphite is in the mix, the softer the lead will be and the blacker the marks it will make.

Next, the graphite mix is pressed into long strips that look like spaghetti. The graphite "spaghetti" is straightened and divided into pencil-sized leads.

The leads are dried in a large oven. Then they are dipped in wax to make writing smoother.

To make the casings that surround the leads, a machine cuts several grooves in a slat, or thin piece, of cedar.

Soft woods like cedar are used in pencils so they will sharpen easily. The leads are placed in the grooves. A second slat is glued tightly over the leads. After the glue dries, another machine saws the slats into pencils. Finally, the pencils are sanded, painted, and fitted with erasers, all set for writing.

How do we get crayons

Here's a clue: Crayons start at a color mill. Let's investigate.

At the color mill, chemicals are mixed to make powdery pigments for the crayons. A pigment gives the crayon its color.

From the mill, we follow the pigments to the crayon factory. Here the pigments are mixed with hot wax.

Next, workers pour the colored wax into small tube-shaped openings in what looks like a table. These are crayon molds. When the wax hardens, the crayons are popped out of their molds. Then a machine covers them in paper labels.

Another machine sorts the crayons so each box gets one of every color. Then the boxes are shipped to stores. Next time you go shopping, track down a box of crayons yourself.

How do we get paper?

To get to the root of this question, we should visit a forest of softwood trees.

Paper is made from cellulose—the woody fibers in the plants. The cellulose in most paper comes from firs and other softwood trees. Every year, foresters plant millions of these trees. The trees grow for thirty to thirty-five years before they are cut down. Then they are sawed into short logs.

Trains carry the logs to a papermaking plant. There a barking drum removes their bark and a chipper grinds them into chips.

Moving belts called conveyors carry the chips into large vats. There the chips are mixed with chemicals and cooked. The chemicals remove the natural glue that holds the wood fibers together. Without the glue, the fibers form a soft mush known as pulp.

Next, a washing machine removes the chemicals from the pulp. In the wash, pulp becomes slurry—a soupy mixture. After that it goes into a bleacher that lightens the natural yellow or brown color. A beater churns the washed and bleached pulp to break up the fibers. Then the beaten pulp flows onto a moving screen. Some water drains through the screen, but the pulp is still very wet. It forms a sheet of paper that is mostly water.

This sheet goes from the screen through squeezing rollers and through very hot drying rollers. When it is fully smooth and dry, the paper is wound into giant rolls.

Amazing! We've gone from a forest of giant trees to a "forest" of giant rolls of paper.

B- 40491
33 1/4

Where do pennies come from ?

It's easy to trace where some pennies come from. They have a clue stamped right on their face. This penny has a *D* below its date. The *D* tells me that the penny comes from the Denver mint.

A mint is a factory where coins are made. The United States has four mints: the one in Denver, Colorado; and others in San Francisco, California; Philadelphia, Pennsylvania; and West Point, New York.

The mints use zinc and copper to make pennies. At one time, pennies were all copper. But today they are made mostly of zinc with a little copper added.

Huge furnaces heat the zinc and copper until they melt. The liquid metal is poured into a bar-shaped mold.

Any rough edges on the bar are shaved off and returned to the furnaces for remelting. Then heavy rollers flatten the bar into a thin strip of metal.

13

The strip goes through a machine that tests its thickness. If the strip is the right thickness for pennies, it continues on to the cutter.

The cutter punches blank coins out of the metal strip, the way a cookie cutter punches cookies out of dough. The blanks are washed, polished, and heated. Then a milling machine gives each blank a raised edge. Raised edges help the designs on the coins to last.

Finally, the blanks go through the coining press, which stamps designs on both sides of the blanks. How powerful is this machine? Imagine how many pounds six elephants weigh. The coining press applies more pressure than that to each square inch of metal.

Part of the design stamped on coins made at the Denver mint is a tiny *D* for "Denver." So the next time you wonder where a penny comes from, take a close look at it. A clue may be staring back at you.

How is ice cream made **?**

To get a scoop, let's go to a dairy plant.

Ice cream starts in this large tub. Here milk, cream, water, sweetener, and most of the other ingredients are mixed. They are pasteurized to kill germs and homogenized to mix thoroughly. The mix ages in the tub for three or four hours.

Great-tasting ice cream has lots of cream—the thick, fatty part of milk. This mix certainly passes the taste test. Now the flavoring is added.

Then the mix is pumped into the ice-cream freezer. The temperature inside the freezer is much colder than freezing. But the ice cream moves through so quickly that it does not freeze solid.

16

The freezer also whips the ice cream with air to make it smooth. After that, the machine adds extras, like chocolate chips. Then the ice cream flows through a spout into cartons.

The cartons are stored in a hardening room. When the ice cream is served, it's hard enough to bend spoons. But if you wait a few minutes, it's just right—smooth, cold, and creamy. Mmm.

Where does peanut butter come from ?

You can't spread a peanut on your sandwich—but you can spread peanut butter. What happens to peanuts between the field and the lunch table?

First, a machine digs up the peanut plants and shakes off the dirt. Another machine separates the pods, or shells, from the leafy tops. Then the peanuts go to a warehouse, where blowers remove the stems.

Next, rollers crack open the pods. Inside each pod are one, two, or even three peanut seeds.

The peanuts roast in a hot oven for up to an hour. Then their thin skins are gently removed by brushes. Next the peanuts go into a grinder with salt and a little oil. This batch will be chunky peanut butter, so it is ground more coarsely than the smooth kind.

In most brands, the oil from the peanuts is homogenized, so that it stays mixed in the peanut butter. But this is not done with natural peanut butter, so the oil comes to the top. You do the mixing before you spread it. Enjoy!

19

What are baseballs made of ❓

Good question! I also wonder what makes a baseball go *Crack!* when the bat hits it. To find our answers, let's visit a factory that manufactures baseballs.

Here we see that a baseball starts with a round cork center. It's made from the bark of the cork oak tree. Cork is light and bouncy. That's the reason the ball can fly so high.

Two layers of rubber are wrapped around the cork. The rubber helps the ball bounce. It also makes that cracking sound when you hit the ball.

Next, yarn is wound again and again around the rubber layers until the ball is the correct size. Then a worker dips the ball in glue. This keeps the yarn from shifting when the bat hits the ball.

A machine stamps out figure-eight-shaped pieces of leather to make the covers. A worker stitches two of these pieces together around each ball. Then the ball is checked for correct size and weight.

Baseballs are pretty sturdy. So don't be afraid to whack that ball with all you've got.

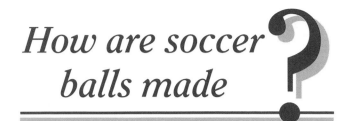

How are soccer balls made ?

We can find out something about a soccer ball just by looking at one. We can see that the cover of the ball has thirty-two pieces.

We can find out even more at a soccer ball factory. There the pieces for the covers are cut from leather or a tough plastic. Then they are lined with cotton. A worker sews pieces together to make the covers—first one half of the cover, then the other. The worker can sew two or three balls a day.

Other workers make bladders that go inside the balls. The workers press warm rubber or a rubberlike material into molds. When the bladders cool, they look like wrinkled balloons. They are put in molds and partly filled with air to smooth them out.

At one time the cover laced shut. But when players hit the ball with their heads, the laces hurt. Now the halves of the cover are placed around a bladder and sewn shut. Next the ball is pumped up, weighed, and measured for roundness. Now it is ready for play. Are you?

How do we get cartoons?

Watching movie or TV cartoons is fun. But making them takes time and work. I'll prove it. Follow me!

Writers and artists plan the words and actions for a cartoon on a storyboard. Then the director draws up a workbook. It gives frame-by-frame directions for making the cartoon. (Have you ever looked at movie film? It is made up of frames, or boxes. Cartoons are shot on movie film. That is why we say the director plans them "frame-by-frame.")

Actors record the cartoon characters' words on tape. Other workers add music and noises, or sound effects. Listening to the sounds helps the artists when they draw. For example, they can make the characters' lip movements match the words.

Many artists work on the drawings for a cartoon. Background artists draw the trees, houses, or other things that set the scene. Key animators draw the characters. Tracers copy the characters onto clear sheets called cels. Painters color the cels.

25

The secret to making cartoons move is to show many, many cels very quickly, one after the other. Each cel shows the character doing just part of an action.

A background picture is pegged to a flat surface. Above the picture is a camera, pointing straight down. One at a time, in order, the cels are placed on top of the background and photographed. Each frame of film shows a different bit of action against the background.

One second of action takes twenty-four frames. So thousands of frames are made for a cartoon. Today computers are used to help make the frames and put them together. When the film rolls, the frames appear so rapidly that things seem to move.

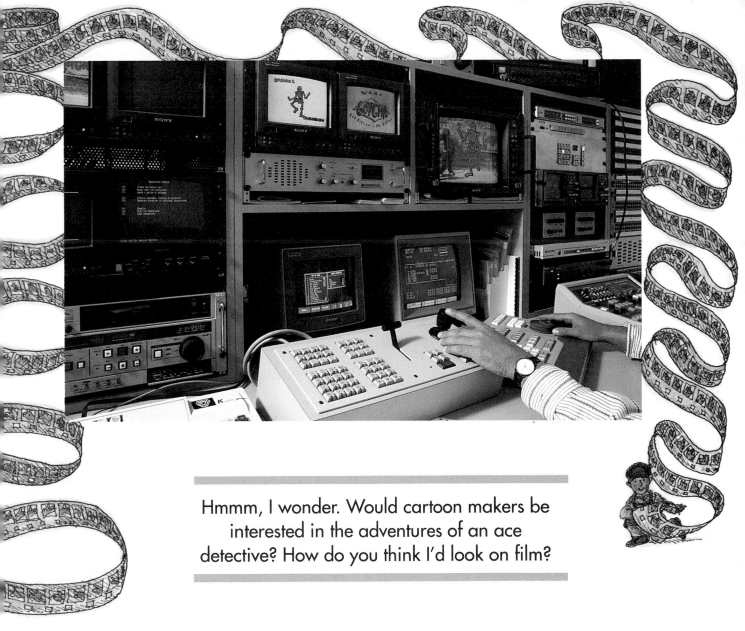

Hmmm, I wonder. Would cartoon makers be interested in the adventures of an ace detective? How do you think I'd look on film?

How do tapes get made?

The answer to this question took a lot of detective work. Here's what I found out.

A sound tape is a long ribbon of plastic coated with tiny particles of iron. A recorder stores sound on tape by rearranging the particles.

The tape is usually inside a cassette, or plastic box. In a new cassette, the tape is wound around a small wheel called the supply reel.

To tape music, you slip a cassette into a recorder. When you turn the recorder on, rubber wheels and small rods called capstans pull the tape along.

The tape moves over the recording head. This head has two sides with a coil of wire around each. It is an electromagnet. Like other magnets, it can move metal, such as iron particles.

The sounds you are recording send electrical signals through the electromagnet. It arranges the iron particles on the tape according to the signals. In this way, the particles store the sounds. The tape then winds around the take-up reel.

Videotapes also come in cassettes and are coated with iron particles. The way they store pictures is similar to the way sound tapes record sounds. Videocassettes record sounds and pictures from your TV set.

To tape a TV program, you turn on your videocassette recorder, or VCR, and slip a videocassette inside. The VCR pulls the tape from the cassette and through the different parts that record the program.

Meanwhile, the television sends electrical signals to the VCR. Inside the VCR, electromagnets in the spinning video head drum pick up the signals that make up the picture. They record the picture in the center of the tape. Next, the audio and control heads store the sound part of the show at the top and bottom of the tape.

Like magic, you now have a tape of your favorite TV program.

Well, it's been an adventure. We've followed a lot of clues and found a lot of answers. We've picked up some facts about how things are made. But this case is never closed. There are always more things to find out about. Any more questions? Just ask Inspector McQ.

To Parents

Children love to ask questions. *All About How Things Are Made,* with special mouse detective McQ, will provide your child with the answers to many common questions children ask about how things are made. These answers will serve as a bridge into learning some important concepts. Here are a few easy and natural ways your child can express feelings and understandings about what Inspector McQ has to say. You know your child and can best judge which ideas she or he will enjoy most.

Give your child pencils, crayons, and a large sheet of paper. Have your child choose one of the "how things are made" articles and create a fanciful picture of a factory that produces the featured product.

Find an old baseball that has seen its last days on the field and help your child take it apart to check the facts in the article about how baseballs are made. Make sure you supervise any slicing of the ball or do it yourself.

Children enjoy cooking projects, and it's fun to have an edible final product! Find a recipe for peanut butter cookies and have your child help you make a batch. Following a recipe lets your child use a variety of measuring devices to create a final product.

Give your child 25 pennies, 5 nickels, 2 dimes, and 1 quarter. Have your child show you how many different ways he or she can find to make a total of 25 cents. You might suggest 25 pennies, or 20 pennies and a nickel, as starters.

Show how animation works by making a cartoon flip book. Take a very small pocket-sized notepad with pages that flip easily through your fingers. Help your child think of one action—a ball rolling down a hill or an arrow shooting through the air, for example. Then your child can draw the action in different stages—one stage per notepad page. Watch how the picture "moves" as you flip through the pages.

To understand the steps in how things are made, begin a project to make sock puppets. First, select a character to make as a puppet. Then talk about the things needed to make the puppet and write a list (socks, buttons, yarn, felt, lace, cloth). Next make a set of directions for what to do. List the steps in order from gathering the materials to using the puppet. Then make the puppet together following the step-by-step directions.